WHAT NOW

AARON ANSTETT

© 2024 by Aaron Anstett

All Rights Reserved.

Printed in the United States of America.
Set in Mrs Eaves XL with LaTeX.

ISBN: 978-1-952386-79-4 (paperback)
Library of Congress Control Number: 2023948037

Sagging Meniscus Press
Montclair, New Jersey
saggingmeniscus.com

*For Wilder
& Theodore
& Lesley, as ever*

WHAT NOW

Say we've always believed magical
tree in rainforest powers to
unite & energize survives all
catastrophe bulldozers lightning please subscribe

to our new true crime
podcast *Capitalism* "criminal mischief" sounds
deceptively fun like "abusing pharmaceuticals"
what now vanishing varnish sun

fingering tinged windows & faces
width & breadth of landscapes
waters sloshing in various vessels
children adrift beds & cradles

13 at yet-to-be-determined
    date an idea first conceived
    & dwelled on in prison
    we will learn to express

17 our message through such visuals
    insinuate positive emotions & happy
    feelings if success does not
    occur verify the signal strength

21 escapees of the 70s who
    like a gritty robbery movie
    love a grim caper heist
    gone wrong like suicide described

25 bankruptcy gradually then all at
    once who would try succeed
    buying a getaway El Camino
    with stack of 20s dye

29 pack pink & who would
    exist as the fabled desert
    island setting for all our
    favorite punchlines *I miss those*

33   *guys* & *We don't go*
     to that one if gas
     station egg salad sandwiches exemplified
     person they'd own a kitchen

37   table neck tattoo windswept handwriting
     signed & who doesn't like
     the voice that lies &
     says OK it's all going

41   to be OK or not
     going to be then adds
     with wink & cackle *Isn't*
     it awful? the invisible hand

45   of the market tickled some
     pinched some lifted many dollars
     night nurse's purse pressed two
     filthy tens into laborer's scarred

49   palm Frenchman with our last
     name illegally sneaked into upstate
     New York from Canada then
     traveled spreading appellation variants &

53   seed the statute of limitations
      & he have long since
      expired what now optical illusion
      one constructs of invisible filament

57   & magnets we double down
      on worst ideas insist enacting
      them improves all lives may
      Wayne LaPierre National Rifle Association

61   head remain haunted always ghosts
      of shot brain become C-suite
      of Dumbass Ideas Ltd. whose
      bon mot make people say

65   *hell no* why does God
      allow sudden things why does
      God allow dry stuffing why
      does God allow muffled rings

69   why does God allow oily
      rags & open flames why
      does God allow no fixed
      address in this comedy snobs

73   meet slobs minds open wide
many disappoint in love &
life but the body that
elaborate contraption complaints department abides

77   dawn underlines the obvious world
still here whatever weather easy
target liquid & light dropping
miles on all these expensive

81   views alleyways birds the color
gravel first-shift vehicles guardrails
quell climbing onramps traffic so
thick it's sound & sight

85   shaking windows we watch it
though our legal recourse against
natural death exactly zero no
constable to enforce the law

89   there ought to exist we
occupy these conveyances even ones
nearest earliest first words briefly
gingerly we lift them whole

93 from bathtub refuge of water
universal solvent each morning tried
tired rising entire into one
being fingers again seizing in

97 work gloves you wore all
winter at job driving to
job driving from in dark
to dark by dark through

101 dark then new old sun
pink & pale on landscape's
details what now in conclusion
the many collisions thankfully failed

105 failing those that actually happened
in summary birds called across
empty air summoned birds began
to cram fullest moon looks

109 like buckshot speed limit sign
moon after moon after mornings
we drove hours car chrome
glinting in sodium light what

113   little we understand of pattern
       & the ephemeral we learned
       from the moon how say
       it not see it spooky

117   moon look look look look
       loopy moon inside the words
       bald heads two full moons
       among things we never knew

121   Latin names for diseases flowers
       clumps of stars looking angular
       like animals good thing these
       portals open ceaselessly like seconds

125   we enter exit either end
       depending honestly Anstett half-assed
       everything mistook clear warnings as
       directives circle of circles contains

129   at center in lounge luxurious
       gloom rusty hinges abandoned amusement
       park rides junkyard backyard once
       found wallet as if flesh

₁₃₃ & brain separate apparatuses first
hands then the thought boxing
15,000 parts daily each ant
trap with sinister eyebrows Anstett

₁₃₇ expressed dismay incredulity outrage detritus
sudden gust pushes missile dotted
line across vandalized land oh
no a spouse must be

₁₄₁ selected robots script the upcoming
season of *Decoy Autocrat* we
focus-group the verse mold it
better then utterly terrible we

₁₄₅ leathered readers queering Kant's contention
sensation can be known artworks
disrupt worm holes in reality
othering rosewater cloaking an odor

₁₄₉ if GG Allin's tattoos spoke
they'd say *Wash me!* imagine
a puppet show of those
criminal onstage antics can we

153 call what he accomplished art
separate work worker one loudmouth
plays plausible mid-tempo R&B but
the accused our guttersnipe Sade

157 as gross dumb & boring
the defendant ladies & gentlemen
was 12 & knew no
better music horses huffing in

161 stalls no longer may one
species going extinct each second
find solace in greatest accounting
of human genitalia on record

165 the word hollered yonder splashy
performer scatological nude audience assaulter
failed self-assassin ascends to heaven
Jerry Lee Lewis & he

169 duet endlessly in hell moron
savant self-described singer committer
aural felony battery saying no
powerful words about same old

173 things what novel expression captures
the glimmering essence pale quintessence
of knockabout roughed-up moon bashed
pancake-powdered panache thunder abrupts

177 lightning scribbles what language lacks
word for pain sounds like
place names market's new sex
game *Derivative Swap* injures many

181 dirty rain lacquers the asphalt
each curt brusque percussive distinct
drop would dampen thatch then
reality show *Hysterical Americans Pursued*

185 *by Animals* premieres upping incidence
of happenstance wash of moonlight
on tombstones sky a barn
slate gray consigned to orphanage

189 we steal to exist return
to mud & grass all
bricks began as government surplus
corrugated outbuildings like wind ripples

193 exhale through harmonica dwindles succinct
    as snapped string eerie lament
    knees & elbows & if
    the angel is named *Heartbreak*

197 let it be named *Heartbreak*
    the river has its direction
    regardless we can talk all
    night long about poor uses

201 of gravity & not even
    begin baby out window one
    that these bodies dormant corpses
    we took such pains feeding

205 bathing clothing wind up there
    claim drawer or prison where
    they piss in your face
    to wake you through inevitable

209 disheveled next second racecar fast
    forward as backward always when
    next we look down our
    own feet propelling us on

213 like some documentary not beautiful
but true now stand beside
a stalled car expression comical
in its frustration & disgust

217 whatever the fiasco's prime mover
we're really in it when
body standing for all bodies
bodies forth body politic arises

221 from ditch when the body
representing everybody face-firsts
between track & train when
the body that remains just

225 one body drifts in wooden
skiff when body of transient
voyager sleeps when all bodies
hunger for nothing when every

229 mouth acquires its proper share
the more than enough when
the plenty goes around then
nobody sleeps in elements accidentally

233 & the voices receive their
say when every cop treats
people better than property any
successful potential applicant allows wind

237 to deliver hither thither forever
thereafter customized resumés all over
loudly applauds boss three times
daily beginning middle & end

241 of shift one sits wondering
if this hasn't already happened
how scenes repeat themselves in
films where they reuse footage

245 refuse edits if this hasn't
already happened your brain seems
up to old tricks again
how scenes repeatedly repeat themselves

249 many scarves pulled from sleeves
your brain up to old tricks
done with mirrors & magnets
so many opulent scarves drawn

253 from sleeves you can step
in the same excrement twice
& if we wake feeling
like something's target who would

257 say any different so much
of us that we must
jump to the other side
of own body & stay

261 there for days remaining teeth
a wreckage with nerve ends
waving hollow sockets all old
lovers in bar discover you

265 what they hold in common
we agree to the suicide
pact then hesitate which worse
more life after this none

269 a gunman breaks in &
makes you eat pastry boxes
full when you look up
from eclairs he's weeping then

273   new crop of snow settles
       some in empty pot outside
       friend's door or phone lines
       sloping five all told to

277   neighbor's house from a pole
       at the edge of property
       blank branches peopled with birds
       when the latest gunman terrorizes

281   shopping mall Anywhere Oklahoma America
       newspaper yellowing rooming house drawer
       grows increasingly distant brake lights
       fade where the fence gave

285   way the driver thought headlights
       the giddy illumination of heaven
       spilled through windshield out over
       the pasture fixed an instant

289   in cows' big eyes world
       where an ant climbed 500x
       its own height the man-at-large
       small on a gurney that

293   current commonplace all things seem
mostly information absences as important
stopgaps scrawl & slang of
blood in gully fog along

297   low-lying enclosures a murky
force we enter & leave
through smallest doorways holes
in my brainless heart show

301   how the road down which
a dog runs as if
struck again & again with
stick we might trap gaunt

305   snake & translate the venom
small doses of medicine faraway
galaxies start looking like carelessness
maybe God forgot to clean

309   weapon of incriminating prints volatile
molecules whose universe expands water
loose on the illustrative illusory
surface its substance switching transfixed

313 by fish their rise swift
as shifting settlement lines smidge
this side of visibility extravagantly
ramshackle where matter just festers

317 pressed to limit of what
may be borne long let
this tree stand for justice
& serendipity & providence battle

321 it out for dollars' worth
of minerals chemicals rare earth
everyone knows someone troubled everyone
in this office wears clothes

325 is sober & has slept
so early ice in urinals
possesses distinct edges maybe soon
we'll look foolish with inky

329 spots of liquid on front
of trousers the dark everywhere
eventually means what it says
rain falling equally on living

333   & dead if you're anything
     like me God help you
     watching worker nail gun shingles
     pneumatic hammering so out-of-synch

337   preceding abstracted sight of her
     moving she looks entirely unconvincing
     mornings I'm all over apey
     superlativest form of the adjective

341   which is infinitiver to die
     or to live too late
     now to devote our time
     to brontology study of thunder

345   what's the form superlativer than
     any other if it's on
     the radio we like it
     listen & we like it

349   if it's on the radio
     enough we love it we
     love to listen to it
     they can't play that one

353 too much it sounds so
good to us we smoke
until the air goes ropy
blue & veins we hadn't

357 known we owned start trembling
at sides of heads like
fidgety drunkards tangling sheets shaking
through uneasy sleep the latest

361 cliché all things more message
than matter less substance than
sensation flickering string of signals
many different cells take turns

365 this may be the world's
most becoming dalliance to sally
forth into worsted trouser
pocket of Larry Fine long-suffering

369 wild-haired fiddle-playing stooge
languid on set between takes
how can he occupy folding
canvas chair that placidly after

373   so many pratfalls those eye-gouging
ax handles the light's lackluster
autumnal as we slip in
past housekey & fan letter

377   folded into quarters & weak
at creases from one Howard
nee Howie a lifelong Missourian
two things cannot be described

381   & one of them's sunset
in the circus of bloodstream
aerialists flash & canter tumblers
quiver & stick thin whipped

385   creatures answer math questions do
as they're commanded some bears
play music other bears dance
to so much plate-spinning dare-deviling

389   that drastic ringmaster's panicked such
fluttery tent flaps horses ridden
bareback that's not blood but
stage paint & sequins not

393 veins but cannons named something
Italian lights sweep & from
my clown-car heart improbable passengers
endlessly emerge hospitals empty no

397 one ill on earth again
& house numbers & street
names rearrange as if cunning
villagers during war fool invaders

401 one must walk doors confirming
location one decided at 14
jail suited few interests stopped
burning things in gutters mostly

405 stopped shoplifting where's some stunt
double to take on these
deprivations & pains long human
history of stillness & motion

409 who coughed years in sunken
sod-lined room who forced
over water in cargo hold
leave it to the buffoon

413   to loudly lambast funeral latecomers
then take the podium guessing
the deceased's most ordinary deeds
slept woke ate & dressed

417   & got undressed glory be
the slyboots insists we left
water & began to walk
was that some trouble God

421   made us full of pranks
to play our pranks on
God birds magnifying transition both
lift aloft & also land

425   on wires legs & feet
steadfast it lessens miracle zero
percent they cannot do otherwise
in lace-curtained patch of light

429   wind we dreamed brought sparks
house burned down & firefighters
with hooks for hands held
hooks in which our papers

433 flared how can anyone remain
that angry & not die
a fury so great cannot
not ruin the days vivify

437 suddenly illustrious nights naturally solemnize
even offer up their way
elegies for those few who
endure through no seeming means

441 of propulsion but will's force
our country where so many
doings of the sad crazed
famous fill miles of screens

445 what now no one lifts
from ground in wind that
sounds like singing but causes
bleeding winter sky dumbed down

449 field no color shape but strips
of dark & light intermittent
rivers tangle our drinking episodic
days so end to end

453 they're palindromes tired we fold
ourselves into self-same beds left
so messy someone foresees such
human joy & suffering then

457 forces all insects one household
to listen to Hound Dog
Taylor demand *Give me back
my wig honey let your*

461 *head go bald* lifts them
wriggling from floor & hovers
each between headphone speakers once
we never knew these lovers

465 now look where we place
our faces the scar on
her palm shone roseate wound
sewn on white wall this

469 infant cricket crawls no longer
than a thumb knuckle fire
has its say how odd
light seems & the sun

473 every fire on earth mirrors
some love how strangers interrupt
private discussions to make themselves
familiar time already I stuck

477 knives in chest walls time
I danced around a little
cup time now I saw
for once the everyday miraculous

481 dead man rolling with laughter
grandfather angry once more once
more it's time I fell
on the ground & flailed

485 kicked the walls & sobbed
soon I'll occupy a village
in a country where I
always face south & my

489 left hand arrives too early
& right arrives too late
before I go I say
it's time I sputtered 100

493 saints' names in black hat
& leaping upon smashed it
vamping on flugelhorn trombone tuba
the showy ways of natural

497 disaster child your mother's battered
her dear brain & memory
with beer on beer killing
messenger swift & fierce all

501 over nation that rampant indexical
on people's minds just ask
them the sun hung in
my rearview from space what

505 seemed level now unbearably steep
some day a last living
nerve end quivers & flicks
no matter how very much

509 then we've come to love
& fear our every cell's
shimmer the thousand thousand globes
of blood as worldwide nerve

513   ends countless grasses & plants
many subaqueous & tensing muscles
jaguars presidents pack mules billionaires
in the asteriskless night air

517   a housefire in daylight ain't
Shangri-la but look slam-bang on
county line under sun fire
redundancy whose gift of gab

521   cunnilingus keeps them in demand
sometimes a man sees all
objects as less substance than
event yet still hopes to

525   make joke in death throes
whether anyone's around to hear
maybe kissing your lover's stomach
the riches all surface areas

529   act in imitation of effigy
creators moved those ungodly amounts
earth into shapes of what
they saw in bent yellow

533 grasses of divided highway offramps
mirror leaves no trace record
expression of landscape & is
useless all dark long but

537 takes periodic pains labors over
trickiest & simplest physics day
& night radio signals without
cease jabber in their frequencies

541 when a fellow driver cuts
me off I'm no prize
I give that fucker finger
I discover in bathtub drain

545 not Atlantis nor the bones
but the emptiness they left
once many footprints going somewhere
in sawdust tools in burlap

549 bag in suit of registered
trademark Blackout the monster's set
of mismatched hands here mountains
look conjured picture of floating

553 world fictive disappearing & immaterial
with distance snow plops clouds'
miniatures we want to find
the place inside us so

557 drunk it cannot stand recalls
nothing where car keys lurk
nor address of anyone helpful
we want the full silo

561 to explode scaring birds whose
wings bear heaven we demand
heaven disassembled & packed in
boxes a forged Vermeer all

565 swollen light on stick figures
ultimate nobodies faces eggshell who
move King Kong jerkily along
one doesn't need to work

569 at a goddamn factory mass-
producing likenesses of president's heads
Halloween masks of exhaustion &
boredom all the earth's narcotized

573 liquids leave a drinker simple
we crawl from water &
fly from ocean that buffet
& sewer maternity ward &

577 charnel house now a man
desires his wife to lick
her own nipples my device
to detect in the singing

581 voices of the insane distinct
messages they look like toy
money the tickets one mother
pulled from her purse to

585 buy food currency of poor
foreign country black & white
eagle & numbers stamped on
pastel paper she tore more

589 slowly when people behind them
whispered & shuffled in line
whose permission required to write
biography of matter all this

593 what-all wind delivers old newspapers
     saying who-knows across storefront
     burglar bars worms in earth
     squinting makes moonlight glinty fearsome

597 musical saws play themselves raw
     one could watch a powerplant
     all night because it is
     low-lying & silver not outlandish

601 as orchids colors of diseased
     innards synonymizing democratizing snow same
     on mansion roofs & garbage
     can lids dear God send

605 capsule we swallow so time
     goes time-lapse everything everything's
     tracery & palimpsest what scars
     & tattoos on scale-model voodoo

609 doll of you who knows
     runs needles through imagine revolver-shaped
     hollow motel bible nightstand booze
     & pill bottles horizontal vertical

613 a communicating doorway communicating vestibule
faces & shoes smeared lit
lightning bugs' phosphorescence what gambit
to amble aimlessly my erstwhile

617 taxi driver told me Aaron
was brother to Moses &
important in the Qur'an dusk
impersonates a mood a mood

621 impersonates the dawn for all
whose T-shirts in mugshots describe
their alleged crimes for those
wearing tavern windbreakers to drunk

625 driving sentencing the derelict electorate
who can't put spent bullet
back in the pistol can't
return oil to the original

629 orange peel can't put miles
back in the vehicle can't
put air back in the
exhale can't put glimmer back

633 in the candle can't put
ink back in the tree
branch can't put bird back
in egg can't put fried

637 eggs back on the menu
if I were king there'd
stand a local thirty seconds
walking from any laundromat quicker

641 in rain with glass brick
windows blocking sun elderly bartender
sullen something steel pedal &
bleak on jukebox fellow inebriates

645 & I could savor long
foolish pulls on our cigarettes
the hand that holds my
heart one day not born

649 yet above my delicately scalpeled
& cracked open sternum under
unforgiving bright lights my eyes
don't see even taped open

653 steadies freckled I'm pale &
fat slit down middle dumb
tattoos on each shoulder &
mermaid above right lung yellow

657 with antiseptic this once let
the body be just body
scrap of map borne along
square inch of river smoothing

661 crumpling rumples then everybody was
kung fu fighting that or
playing with increasingly unwilling partners
got your nose some demanded

665 where is Thumbkin that was
me standing naked in front
of strangers teeth marks on
my shoulder unable to hide

669 anything me a series of
lights & darks the teacher
says I'm now divided into
spaces & hollows this body

673   I use for everything new
sudden study in line composition
logically follows I work hard
doing nothing takes up all

677   my strength sitting one position
moving so little I could
be asleep or thinking something
worth money instead of everything

681   loss persistently & diligently undoes
& how nervous I am
to move & how little
heaven endures in the world

685   ponder now the inevitable ignobility
of possessing physiognomy some day
removed from the official record
like stones from quarry molecules

689   travel without papers any identification
a walker who loves swaying
undersides powerlines & branches lit
by passing ambulances consider also

693 long lineage family tree
one flower Podunk from which
a savior sprang jump no
higher in vest of feathers

697 though zero evidence supports it
memory serves as a kind
of cartilage let us imagine
what dogs dream while yipping

701 & shivering in sleep we
will publish the veins of
this maple leaf across bare
air the hieroglyph that looks

705 like roots inverted or first
draft blueprint of a tree
we will print this with
lasers & fireworks I am

709 about to commit a crime
if you require articulable suspicion
I wash away all evidence
with soapy water again &

713   again the so-so poems end
again & again elegant object
in shape of starburst vibrates
quietly in warehouse now my

717   daily allowance of banalities includes
that strange phrase "realistic fiction"
in languorous sentence one grows
impatient awaiting arrival of point

721   we fear may never surface
blood from lip as you
kiss it coppery what now
we discern in palm's lineaments

725   even strongest materials pull apart
subject to force & load
after scuffle with officer remember
how it felt to feel

729   sun on face see gleam
on edge of nickel I'm
half in love with shadows
of sparrows their skittery flurry

733 the wavery penumbra what forecasts
their random telegrams dash-dash-dash dot-dot-dash
I want predictions to polka-dot
all continents as penance for

737 my duncery we've made it
through many worse scrapes than
birth when the low-cost final
expense solicitors call I talk

741 at length about my grand
burial plans for see-through racecar-
theme mobile crematorium in which
my cadaver that flameout's rotisseried

745 as loved ones watch shocked
until they hang up or
ask do you know these
implausible facts about animals vanishing

749 easily envisioned I eke in
alley tawdry milieu haw hoo
the metaphor for metaphor remains
dump truck carryall tenor vehicle

753 among the actual's squalid qualia
the heart feels wrong-sized weird
colossal bonsai minuscule castle herd
akin to skin a kindness

757 here in the precarity bodily
being the poem progresses until
first line's import erodes I
sat outside & listened crickets

761 chirruped cheer-ups Dopplered like sirens
circled overtoned when the pills
commandeer we have great powers
see the future if tomorrow

765 didn't block it doorway oaf
the visible a force loose
in the world who reconciles
the specters this & that

769 once a mother listened all
night in static between stations
for voice to teach her
to live she never heard

773 it I made this up
my mother sounds happy for
once I clicked my teeth
on cocaine in stranger's apartment

777 cracked dinner plate rain glaciers
on long crawl across great
plains forced animals indoors to
bear fur nurse young remember

781 gas station sign missing letters
offering fat & friendly service
asleep holding own shoulders please
do not break the chain

785 of evidence the form around
all mysteries remain mysteries friend
in universe dollhouse crime scene
blood stain splatter applied painstakingly

789 with single strand horsehair brush
like emetic when attempting comedic
material my vanity plate reads
Eyelids my invisible ink tattoos

793 say *Night night* when it
comes to awful ideas I'm
completist death like when fish
swims from skillet to river

797 away swims dinner fast food
on so many last meal
requests maybe organize poetry books
by suicide method sozzled gods

801 through tavern doors enrapt in
ball scores childish above beers
weep foolishly about umpire calls
through afternoons wide as August

805 astraddle stools cast lots rattle
dice in leather cups spill
digits across cigarette burns along
bar tops fishing's two hungers

809 connected by a line see
now what time has done
call weirdo environmental artists commission
them size all of Iowa

813 for tuxedo pants by the purchasing
power vested in me buying
a magnum of champagne stretches
here to Japan setting glittering

817 chalice in each empty hand
seen from distance two men
grappling might well be dancing
Texas warehouse hundreds of pallets

821 of math books now suddenly
open themselves to same story
problem regarding bullet's trajectory extravaganzas
avalanches panoramas in patches splashes

825 substantial my son the philosophy
minor says this semester he's
studying epistemology I ask how
he knows tuition he says

829 the atoms that spin us
might fly from their hinges
or trees collapse as if
fashioned from ash not earthquake

833 or bomb pure bad luck
odd happenstance clouds lumber past
in most ungainly manner echoes
in air vaults voices filling

837 elevator shafts darkness in desk
drawers motherfuckers navigate carnival midway
flattening grasses expressions pockmarks punctuate
what was a singular mind

841 now pink mist Jesus wept
who wouldn't feet-first Anstett bowling
pins ninjas boomerangs in air
like Bollywood CGI Anstett get

845 down from there vowels glissando
glide like clothes over skin
after each salvo rub placebo
salve on wounds small as

849 curios useless & thorough we
apprehend no more than comprehend
what faces in paintings think
scientists zero in on sea's

853   true color tied to bullet
sparrow feather zooms we leap
over thin river with legs
longer than rain what prayer

857   can prayers have transmitted
all this signal-bombarded air light
a luxury this penis extender
works night & day extending

861   penises greater distances than penises
extended previously these were atoms
that are my eyes seeing
surface area of all 10,000

865   things newsprint pinned to fencing
by pre-literate wind tattoo vernacular
name of each body each
body part or better wrongly

869   "Arm" on ear et cetera
muscles jumpy in jailing skin
imagine the field through which
animals move dark vague shapes

873   Dolly Parton save us Dolly
        Parton run for president Dolly
        who said people call me
        a dumb blonde but I'm

877   not dumb & I'm not
        blonde in America little happens
        poverty evictions life & death
        sentences without someone turns buck

881   Dolly funded pandemic vaccines Dolly
        we don't deserve you Dolly
        never leave us Dolly Parton
        will never lead us astray

885   unlike billionaire criminals with big
        ideas about how the world
        should work & teams building
        rockets to escape burning planet

889   one responded to the post
        Holland has tulips what does
        your country have mobility issues
        diabetes too many shooting sprees

893   wind traveled such wavy directions
to loft broad daylight unkempt
man's head hat that skittered
& rolled through street grit

897   to land on crown beneath
parked squad car you lay
on asphalt in T-shirt jeans
to fetch & gingerly between

901   fingertips return it thank you
word traveled such distances to
lift weest dark hours one
spirit thank you we've heard

905   everyone's doing their best even
presidents executing by drone strike
small children light traveled such
distances to shine on smile

909   first the pianist's fingers levers
& hammers trees all wood
wood was even sheet music
before ink then ink all

913 its water the mouth that
 says nothing but breath one
 long metrical sentence pre-emptive
 obit errata for "shallow grave"

917 "wooded pasture" for "difficult" "idiosyncratic"
 no escaping the domain in
 land overrun with animatronic vermin
 this space available business establishments

921 simmer firefighters lean on saloon
 rail leaves ashes on boots
 intercept the squawk box signals
 fizzle spit hissing staticky read

925 for umpteenth time livid descriptions
 whispers exit faces in smallest
 cartoon text balloons vomiting milk
 cat back curved as parentheses

929 sun's portrait on eyelids all
 orchards eerie as octopi icy water
 presto a message amen someone
 anon says strobe-lit getting ill

933 slow motion attended by professionals
flowers blossom breakneck pace better
request written permission from commissioner
major league baseball to legally

937 recall good game in dream
one where all siren factories
close for lack of emergencies
follow shimmying cinema verité-color dump

941 truck rubble uphill no fear
wishing yourself blade of grass
or bird not knowing solitary
word but pointing outside map

945 border each thing's ingredient list
x-number atoms daily allowance struggle
what now sweet Jesus what
now merciful Allah what now

949 unequalled Vishnu doctor in joke
tells terminal patient good news
Did you see the beautiful
receptionist redhead at front desk

953 *I'm screwing her Why* asks
patient *are you telling me
this* doctor answers *I'm telling
everyone* I'm telling everyone what

957 my new condensed matter Algerian
physicist pal big for Japan
average for America said when
I mentioned giant Kamakura Buddha

961 *Why should I travel 90
minutes by train to see
some fat fuck* my friend
asked *I own a mirror*

Photo by Lesley Ginsberg

Aaron Anstett is the author of eight previous collections, including most recently *This Way to the Grand As-Is: New and Selected Poems* and *Late-Stage Everything*. A technical writer and editor, he currently occupies a subway-car-size room near the Komaba-tōdaimae station on the University of Tokyo campus with his wife, Lesley, though they are due to return to Colorado in late 2024.

Also By Aaron Anstett

Late-Stage Everything (2022)

This Way to the Grand As-Is: New and Selected Poems (2020)

Please State the Nature of Your Emergency (2017)

Moreover (2016)

Insofar as Heretofore (2014)

Each Place the Body's (2007)

No Accident (2005)

Sustenance (1997)

www.ingramcontent.com/pod-product-compliance
Lightning Source LLC
Chambersburg PA
CBHW020959090426
42736CB00010B/1394